BRITAIN IN OLD PH

TIPTON

A SECOND SELECTION

JOHN BRIMBLE & KEITH HODGKINS

SUTTON PUBLISHING LIMITED

Sutton Publishing Limited
Phoenix Mill · Thrupp · Stroud
Gloucestershire · GL5 2BU

First published 1997

Copyright © John Brimble & Keith Hodgkins,
1997

Cover photographs:
front: Mitchard's coal boat outside the Beehive,
1962; *back*: Tan Sad workers and their families
in Toll End Road.

British Library Cataloguing in Publication Data
A catalogue record for this book is available from the
British Library.

ISBN 0-7509-1376-2

Typeset in 10/12 Perpetua.
Typesetting and origination by
Sutton Publishing Limited.
Printed in Great Britain by
Ebenezer Baylis, Worcester.

To our Black Country forefathers, who made it all possible.

FOREWORD

Although they readily admit that it is not the most beautiful place in the world, Tiptonians have always displayed an intense loyalty to their town. A fierce pride has been engendered by two hundred years of industrial activity which has produced skills and achievements of national, if not international, significance.

Tipton people, even those in exile, like to boast of their roots in the town and of their connections with its contributions to the wealth of this country down the years.

But Tipton's self-esteem received a severe blow when it lost its separate civic identity with local government reorganization in 1966. This book reaffirms that identity by recording the past through photographs and ensuring their survival for posterity. I hope that it will keep the name of Tipton to the fore and reinforce the collective pride of its inhabitants.

The Rt. Hon. Betty Boothroyd MP
Speaker, House of Commons

CONTENTS

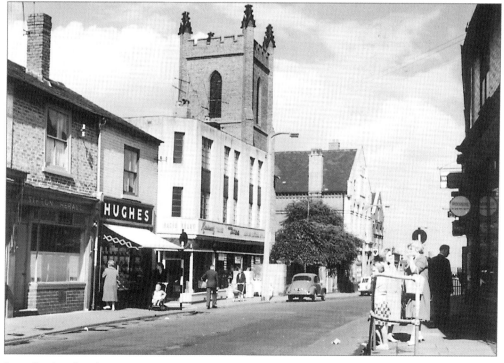

St Paul's Church and Owen Street, 1962.

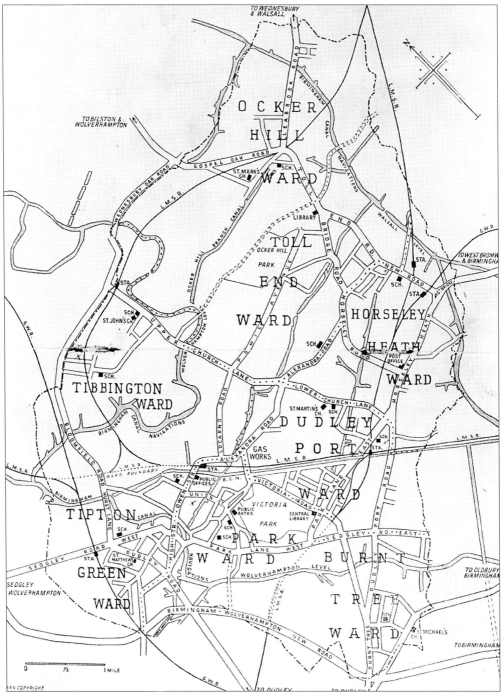

The street map that appeared in the Tipton Urban District Council handbook of 1935 and showed the canal system at its greatest extent before the closures of the postwar era began. Also marked are the boundaries of the eight constituent wards, each of which returned three representatives, giving the town a council of twenty-four members. At this time Tipton covered an area of 2,167 acres and had a population of 35,184.

INTRODUCTION

Tipton is a widely spread district comprising several distinct communities, including Tipton Green, Princes End, Toll End, Ocker Hill, Horseley Heath and Burnt Tree. The inhabitants of these separate areas have always been proud Tiptonians, yet with a fierce sense of belonging to their own separate locality within Tipton. Princes End might just as well be a hundred miles away from Burnt Tree to hear the locals talk, but if called upon to defend Tipton against any criticism they would all stand solidly next to each other. This cohesion is quite remarkable and not easily understood by outsiders.

This intense pride appears to have been engendered by migrants from other areas of the country who flocked to Tipton in the nineteenth century to work in the thick coal seams and ironworks for which Tipton was well known. Workers came from Wales, Ireland, Shropshire, Gloucestershire and Somerset and tended to settle in homes and streets close to each other. For instance, there were several Welsh families at Princes End, many West Country families in Wood Street, while Old Cross Street was the stronghold of the Irish. Pockets of localized independence were formed and this tended to perpetuate itself over the decades.

The origins of Tipton were at Summerhill where the parish church (St John as it is today) had ancient foundations. On becoming dilapidated and too small for the growing population, a new church was built in 1797 on a relatively isolated site near Horseley Heath that was well away from Tipton Green, the area that was to become the principal business centre and commercial thoroughfare. Thus, the parish church never became a focal point around which further development took place.

During the nineteenth century massive expansion of the coal and iron trades resulted in a growth of population from 4,000 to 30,000 and an amazing scene of industrial activity was created which was described in Pigot's Directory of Staffordshire in 1842:

. . . Although what may be called Tipton does not extend in breadth nor length more than three miles; yet such is the sinuosity of the Birmingham Canal that it exceeds 20 miles [an overstatement] within the limits of the parish and affords, in connection with its collateral branches, a communication with almost every line of inland navigation; and the produce of its mines and manufactures is conveyed to many of the principal towns in the kingdom. The coal mines are said to be inexhaustible, the strata averaging 30 feet in thickness; and iron works are on a most extensive scale. Nails and hinges are made in great quantities, as are fire irons, fenders, boilers and steam engines, with many other articles from iron: and cannons of large calibre are manufactured at Gospel Oak Foundry. There are also boat building and timber yards, and a considerable manufactory of soap; while clay of a superior quality, obtained here in great plenty, is employed in the manufacture of fire bricks. The land here, from the great value of the mineral treasures it contains, has been known to be rented so high as £1,000 an acre . . .

The centres of population grew up on the principal roads which formed a rough circle around the parish, with the land in the centre given over to coal mining and large ironworks. In time these communities grew and merged to form continuous strips of development such as that from Great Bridge through Horseley Heath and Dudley Port to Burnt Tree, but the patterns of use in the central area did not begin to change until after the First World War with the construction of housing and newer industries away from the original settlements.

Modern Tipton, therefore, has evolved into a town without a discernible nucleus and is in fact a collection of communities with one common thread, that being the name. This book attempts to visit each of the various constituent communities separately to see how they have each contributed to the story of Tipton.

Five of the sections start with an extract from the 6 inch to 1 mile Ordnance Survey map of 1921, capturing the landscape at a time when the mining and iron industries were in decline, but before the original communities had begun to be dispersed by the first slum clearances. From the early 1920s the construction of council estates, at quite low density, led to a gradual suburbanization of the old mining areas and remaining pockets of farmland. Subsequent reclamation schemes, particularly since the 1960s, have removed all evidence of Tipton's vital role in the exploitation of the once mighty South Staffordshire coalfield.

BLOOMFIELD, PRINCES END & TIBBINGTON

Factory Basin and its unique lifting bridge four months after the closure of the goods yard, August 1968. The bridge was installed in 1922 to facilitate vehicular access to the area between the two basins, and could be winched up by hand to allow boats to reach the inner basin. It was dismantled in 1971 and taken to the Staffordshire County Museum at Shugborough for preservation. In 1977 it was transferred to the newly established Black Country Museum, where it was re-erected as a working exhibit across the entrance to the museum's own canal basin, less than a mile from its original site.

The plaque in the grounds of the British Rolling Mills (now Firsteel Cold Rolled Products) commemorating the historic Bloomfield engine. This was unveiled by Lord Northesk on behalf of the Newcomen Society on the same day as the company opened new laboratories, 27 May 1959. The engine was the first to embody the separate condenser invented by James Watt and was constructed by the firm of Boulton and Watt for the proprietors of Bloomfield Colliery, where it was put to work pumping water from the mine workings. It represented a milestone in the development of engineering technology without which the Industrial Revolution could not have progressed.

Bloomfield Infants School, September 1968. The school opened in 1890 and originally provided accommodation for 180 children. Being considered too small by modern standards, the distinctive building was closed and demolished in the mid-1970s.

A footpath to the left of the school crossed the Dudley to Wolverhampton railway on a footbridge, from which this view was obtained, 15 February 1958. On the left is the busy Princes End goods yard being shunted by a Great Western pannier tank loco and on the right the repair works of the South Staffs Wagon Co. Ltd. The boundary between Tipton and Coseley Urban District ran to the right of the wagon sidings but was re-drawn tight to the edge of the railway in 1966 with local government re-organization. Thus the westernmost edge of Tipton was sliced off and transferred to the newly enlarged Dudley County Borough.

The Hipkins family at the turn of the nineteenth century. Edward Hipkins (1818–1910), the old man in the centre of the picture, was a candle manufacturer and tallow merchant with premises at Bloomfield Road. He was a devout Methodist following a long family tradition, being associated with Bloomfield Methodist Chapel for many years. He was a circuit steward for fifty years and one of the original members of the Tipton Local Board of Health. To his left sits his son Daniel Hipkins JP, who was also prominent in the religious and public life of the town.

Daniel Hipkins JP (1841–1938), a leading figure in the public life of Tipton in the late nineteenth and early twentieth centuries. He was chairman of the Tipton Local Board of Health 1889–94, then, when this authority was superseded by the Tipton Urban District Council in 1895, he became the first chairman. He was to hold the latter office for no fewer than six terms. His influence over Tipton at that time was considerable. He followed in the family animal-fat business and was a pioneer in the manufacture of 'Butterine', a product which was later to become 'Margarine'. He had business premises in Albion Street and lived in a large house, now demolished, named Ivy House at the corner of High Street and Dudley Road. He died in 1938 at the age of ninety-seven years.

St Joseph's Mission Church in Newhall Street became the focus of St John's parish life between 1913 and 1921, when the mother church was closed for repairs necessitated by mining subsidence. Little else is known about the mission except that some time before the Second World War it was acquired by W.G. Allen and Sons, who developed the site as a company social club.

An aerial view of Princes End, *c.* 1930. This was issued as an advertising postcard by W.J. Tranter Ltd, lubricating oil manufacturer, whose premises can be seen in the centre of the picture. St John's Church can be seen in the top left, next to the then recent council-housing development, which included St John's Road, Summerhill Road, Tozer Street and Turner Street. On the extreme right is Newhall Street with the St Joseph's Mission and Princes End Baptist church. Note the great extent of derelict land, nearly all of which was later to be reclaimed for council housing. In 1948 Tipton still had 470 acres of derelict land, 22 per cent of its total area.

Tom Genner, caretaker of the Princes End
Baptist church, Newhall Street, with his wife
Polly outside their small house at the rear of the
church, *c.* 1910. The Princes End branch
railway ran at the rear of the house which can
be seen, together with the church and adjacent
Sunday school, on the right of the aerial
photograph on page 11.

A narrow gauge double bogie sugar cane car, probably bound for the West Indies, manufactured by
W.G. Allen & Son, August 1951. This firm, located at the junction of Princes End High Street and Bradley
Lane, actually within the boundaries of Coseley UDC, was established in about 1850. They specialized
initially in mining equipment, particularly underground railway tubs, and later developed light railway
rolling stock of all descriptions, including much for export to all parts of the world.

Diagonally opposite Allen's on the corner of Bloomfield Road and Newhall Street stands the Royal Hotel, a Mitchell's and Butler's pub until it was purchased by Holden's Brewery of Woodsetton in 1977. Eades Drug Stores was one of the small chain of family-run chemist's shops in Tipton, with other outlets at various times in Dudley Port, Bridge Road and Owen Street. Note the flamboyant wooden bracket on Cresswell's shop front. All these buildings with the exception of the pub were demolished in the 1970s.

The Seven Stars pub and adjacent premises of John Seedhouse and Sons in High Street, Princes End, August 1968. Seedhouse's brewed on this site from 1912 to about 1960 and continued as wine and spirit merchants with their own cooperage until closing in 1993. The Seven Stars was renamed the Great Bear in the early 1970s and closed in about 1980. The site was redeveloped as a supermarket in 1995.

Princes End Joint School headmaster, Mr R.G. Turley, seated right, and staff with the school football team, *c.* 1930. The 'Joint' in the name referred to the fact that the school was built as a joint venture in 1913 by Tipton and Coseley Councils, being close to the boundary between the two authorities. The school is still known to older Tiptonians as 'the Joint'.

The Union Inn, 1958. Being located on the north side of Princes End High Street, this pub, the Seven Stars and numerous other dwellings and shops lay over the Tipton boundary in Coseley Urban District, although all these premises carried a Tipton address. The Union Inn was demolished in about 1970 and replaced by a new pub called the Lagoon.

Princes End signal box and level crossing in Upper Church Lane, July 1969. The old gates were replaced by automatic barriers in the early 1970s. Following the closure of the line in 1980 the track bed was converted into a public walkway, creating a useful pedestrian shortcut down to Ocker Hill.

Princes End station, on the branch line from Bloomfield Junction to Wednesbury, 25 May 1957. The line was opened by the LNWR in 1863, but closed in 1890 owing to competition from the Dudley to Wednesbury steam trams which passed along the adjacent High Street. The service was restored in 1895 and extended to connect with Dudley Port, but only lasted until 1916 when it became a victim of wartime economies. The station platforms survived and the line continued in freight-only use until 1980 but saw the occasional enthusiast's special train, for example the one seen here. It had been organized by the Midland Area of the Stephenson Locomotive Society and was hauled by the former LMS tank loco No. 42627.

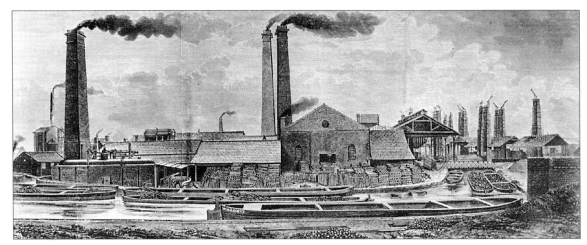

The ironworks of William Millington and Co., *c.* 1873. These were established in 1821 off Upper Church Lane next to the site of the old church (now St John's). A contemporary description stated: 'This establishment consists of 16 puddling, five mill and one annealing furnaces, four mills, a forge and one helve. The production capacity is 200 tons a week consisting of merchant bar iron, plates, straps, angle iron, shoe tip iron, horse shoe and rivet iron, cable and chain iron of nearly every size, shape and variety.' Some 150 men were employed at the factory.

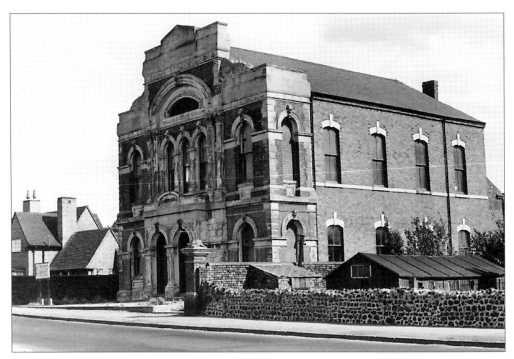

Gospel Oak Wesleyan Chapel, High Street, Princes End, September 1968. It was erected in 1876 at a cost of £4,780 and could accommodate 525 worshippers. It replaced an earlier structure of 1811. The Millington family of Summerhill Ironworks were ardent philanthropic supporters of the chapel. The last service was held on 31 March 1987, and the building was demolished in the following May.

A parcel train hauled by the 'Jubilee' class loco No. 45670 *Howard of Effingham*, heads up the steep bank from Ocker Hill towards Princes End, 1961. The bridge in the distance carried the railway over the Old Main Line canal, by then abandoned. The open land on the right was known as the Glebefields, signifying church land in the distant past, and was developed for council housing in the 1960s. The pigeon loft encroaching on to the railway is an interesting feature of this picture.

St John's Church football team, 1947–8. At this time they played in the Cradley Heath League. The players changed in the church clubroom then walked to their pitch some distance away 'next to the cut', on what is now the Glebefields estate. The vicar of St John's at this time was the Revd John Oldham Johnson.

St John's Church in a ruined state and surrounded by the smoking chimney-stacks of colleries and ironworks, 1837. Originally the parish church (St Martin's), it was abandoned in 1797 when it became too small for the expanding population and the new parish church was erected in Lower Church Lane. The old church was rebuilt and rededicated to St John in 1854. The tower, which still stands, could possibly date from the thirteenth century, making it the oldest structure existing in Tipton.

St John's Church tower (or St Martin's as it then was) underwent a rebuilding in the seventeenth century, when this sundial, with its semicircular pediment, was set into the stonework on the south wall. The inscription reads 'this steeple was built anno domini 1689, John Nightingale, William Clare, Church Wardens.' The tower is 30 ft in height and constructed of the local coal-measures sandstone known as Peldon stone.

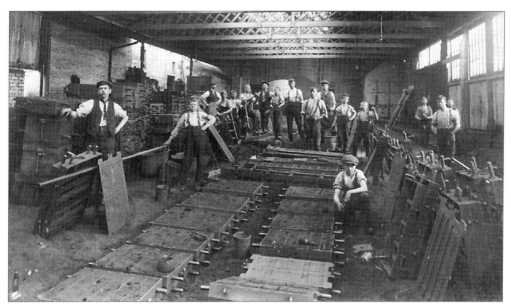

The foundry of Charles Lathe and Co., *c.* 1920. It was established in 1872 in Upper Church Lane, Summerhill, and grew to specialize in the manufacture of cast-iron fire grates and kitchen ranges. In the 1920s, when 'blackleaded' iron grates were going out of fashion, Lathe's built a set of brick bottle kilns in order to make ceramic tiles for more modern styles of grate.

CLACO GRATES
IDEAL TYPES FOR ANY HOUSE

COMBINATION GRATES
(ALL TYPES).
"KUXWEL" GRATES.
"MIDGET" GRATES.
MANTEL REGISTERS.
TILE REGISTERS.
INTERIORS.
RUSTLESS BOILERS, Etc.

"CLACO" TILE WORKS
HIGH CLASS
TILE SURROUNDS,
WALL TILING, MOTTLES,
ANTIQUE COLOURS
in all varieties and sizes.
ALL TILE SITTING ROOM
OR BEDROOM FIREPLACES.

CHAS. LATHE & CO. LTD.,
MOAT FOUNDRY, TIPTON, STAFFORDSHIRE

Lathe's used the trade name CLACO (an acronym of their title) and this advertisement shows one of their latest combination grates which had taken the place of the old cast-iron ranges, 1930. The stove enamelled finish with ceramic tile panels and hearth meant the end of the tedious job of blackleading. The move away from domestic solid fuel appliances in the 1960s brought about the closure of the company at the end of that decade.

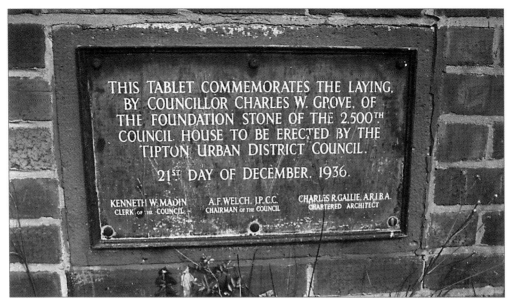

From 1919 one of the main priorities of Tipton Council was the re-housing of people displaced by slum-clearance schemes and large areas of derelict mining land were reclaimed for the construction of council-housing estates. One of the largest of these, developed in the mid-1930s, was the Tibbington estate – which happened to include the 2,500th dwelling built by the council, at 68 Central Avenue. This was considered to be a civic achievement worthy of this special foundation stone.

The Tibbington estate was quite isolated from the old centres of population and so a large public house named the Tibbington was provided in Central Avenue. Designed by the architects Scott and Clark of Wednesbury, it was opened on 21 June 1938 shortly before Tipton's incorporation as a borough and the town's coat of arms still hangs in one of the rooms. The name Tibbington is actually the ancient name for Tipton, appearing as 'Tibbintone' in the Domesday survey of 1086. Curiously, the Tibbington estate earned itself the nickname 'Abyssinia', possibly because its construction coincided with Italy's invasion of that country in 1935.

Locarno Road Schools, 1955. This site was opened on 27 October 1938 by Councillor Albert Parker (Chairman of the Education Committee) and Councillor W.J.W. George (Deputy Charter Mayor). The buildings provided accommodation for 500 juniors, 300 infants, together with 40 nursery places, and were constructed on two storeys to conserve as much of the site as possible for playing space. This picture was taken from the aqueduct which carried the Old Main Line canal over Central Avenue.

The staff of the newly opened Locarno Road Schools pose for an official photograph in the assembly hall. The schools opened just a few weeks after Tipton was granted its Charter of Incorporation as a Borough and the new coat of arms is proudly displayed on the wall. Seated in the centre is the headmaster, Mr J.H. Laugher, and to his right, Mr H.R. Longford, who later became headmaster of Tipton Green Schools.

The Old Main Line canal looking east from Summerhill bridge towards Ocker Hill, 1955. On the left are the houses in Moat Road, and in the distance the two cooling towers of Ocker Hill power station (a third was built in 1956) and the chimney-stack of the BCN workshops. This short stretch of canal and the Ocker Hill branch, which served the BCN workshops, were officially abandoned in 1955.

The Triplex Foundry originated in Toll End in the 1920s, but moved to its present site in Upper Church Lane in the early 1930s. As with Lathe's, one of the principal products of the firm was fire grates, a fact well advertised by this Thorneycroft lorry photographed when brand new in the mid-1930s. The location is thought to be in West Bromwich as the body was built by Fred Smith and Son of that town.

BURNT TREE, DUDLEY PORT & TIVIDALE

A Birmingham Corporation no. 74 bus on the Birmingham–Dudley service passing the Jolly Brewer pub at Burnt Tree, 1968. The houses on the right disappeared in the late 1970s, while the pub survived a little longer, being demolished in 1980. The name Burnt Tree is unusual and is thought to have originated from a tree that acted as a parish boundary marker and was damaged by lightning.

The brewhouse at the rear of the Jolly Brewer public house at Burnt Tree, 1978. For many years the licensee of this pub was William George, a long-serving member of Tipton Council, who became the first Deputy Mayor of the Borough of Tipton in 1938. A fervent supporter of incorporation for Tipton, he always said that if Tipton ever achieved borough status he would change the name of the pub to the Borough Arms. However, when Tipton finally achieved borough status the pub name remained unchanged. The photograph was taken from the car park of Ney Court, a block of flats built on the site of a large Victorian house called The Beeches. The flats were constructed in the mid-1970s by the Waterloo Housing Association and perpetuated the name of the French soldier, Marshal Ney.

The no. 74 and no. 87 tram routes met on the Dudley side of Burnt Tree junction after crossing the Birmingham New Road, which opened in 1927. A large traffic island was constructed here in the early 1950s, which now marks the southernmost point of Tipton. It is also Tipton's highest point at 550 ft above sea level. The photograph is dated 6 September 1938.

Tividale Road, like Princes End High Street, straddled the Tipton boundary. Before 1966, the right-hand side of the road to a point just past Barnett Street was in Dudley, beyond which a small triangular piece of Tipton claimed St Michael's Church. Thereafter lay Rowley Regis borough. After 1966, the boundaries were rationalized and the area to the right, including the church, became part of Warley County Borough. Despite the loss of St Michael's in 1984, this picture from 1955 presents a familiar scene.

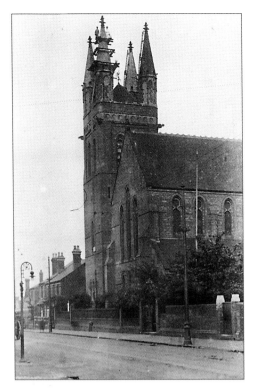

Tividale was formed into an ecclesiastical parish from parts of Rowley Regis and Tipton in 1879. The parish church of St Michael's was built in 1877–8 at a cost of £11,390. It was described as an edifice of brick in the Early English style, consisting of chancel, nave aisles, north and south porches and a western tower with pinnacles containing one bell. An organ was erected in 1891 and there was seating for 750 people. The church contained a window depicting the Virgin Mary beneath which was the legend 'Queen of the Black Country'. The photograph shows repair work being carried out on the pinnacles in about 1910.

The Patronal Festival march leaving St Michael's Church and moving along Tividale Road in the direction of Dudley, 1936. This was led by Roger Moss, who is swinging the incense. Immediately behind him carrying the candlestick is local butcher Henry Hall (see page 48). The Anglo-Catholic regalia is a reminder that St Michael's was always regarded as High Church. The Gate Hangs Well public house is seen in the background.

The Gate Hangs Well, Tividale Road, 1969. The pub had a sign in the form of a gate which bore the ditty 'The gate hangs well, And hinders none, refresh and pay, and travel on'. Sadly, travellers are no longer refreshed there as the pub was closed and demolished in the mid-1970s.

An open-balconied tramcar heads towards Burnt Tree along Dudley Road West, 12 April 1939. This route opened to steam-hauled trams from Birmingham to Dudley via Smethwick and Oldbury in 1885, and was electrified in 1904. It was the last section of tramway to operate in the Black Country, closing on 30 September 1939, after which the no. 87 service was taken over by Midland Red buses. None of the buildings in this picture still exist. To the right of the tram in the distance is the Waggon and Horses public house, rebuilt in the late 1970s on the corner of Groveland Road.

Another no. 87 tram heads towards Oldbury having just passed Tividale Street, 6 January 1938. The location is almost the same as the previous picture. Tividale played an important part in the Black Country tramway system as the principal workshops were located here between 1907 and 1930; the entrance tracks to the depot can be seen branching off and crossing the pavement on the right. The overhead gear remained in place for feeder purposes from a sub-station in the depot yard until the end of tram services.

The funeral procession of the Revd Joseph Cash Matthews, Vicar of St Michael's Church since 1926, moves along Gate Street with the church tower in the background, September 1960. The cortège is headed by master of ceremonies, Edwin Taylor, son of the Tipton Borough Librarian, Alexander W. Taylor. The middle clergyman of the group of three nearest the coffin is the Revd Alan Thomas, Vicar of St Martin's.

The Revo brass band leads the Sunday school anniversary procession of the Tividale Street Methodist Church and turns from Dudley Port back into Tividale Street at the end of the march, early 1950s. The Revo Electric Company of Groveland Road was a major manufacturer of domestic electrical appliances, which at its peak covered 40 acres and employed over 2,000 people.

The temporary wooden porch across the doorway and the blanked-out headlights of the Wolseley car suggest that this photograph of Cottage Spring Pub in Dudley Port was taken just before or just after the outbreak of the Second World War. This neat 1920s pub stands next to 'the City', a grandly named alley which links Dudley Port and Coneygre Road. The Cottage Spring closed in 1996.

Dudley Port took its name from the wharves and warehouses which grew up around the spot where the main road to Dudley crossed the Old Main Line canal, opened in 1772, and literally became 'Dudley's Port'. These origins were also reflected in the name of the Old Port Hotel, built next to the canal bridge. The hotel is seen here in the 1890s offering Connolly's home-brewed ales, although this would not have pleased Joey Bough, a local temperance campaigner who ran the adjoining chapel.

The Old Port Hotel closed in the mid-1970s and by 1968 has been converted, together with the chapel, into a motor repair garage. The old humpback bridge was rebuilt in the early 1960s, but came in for criticism as the hump appeared to have been accentuated. The buildings were demolished in 1979, but the name has been perpetuated in the nearby housing development called Old Port Close.

Old houses in Dudley Port, probably dating from the 1830s, on the west side of the main road between Fisher Street and 'the City' photographed in the mid-1930s, possibly as an official record before their demolition. The site remained empty until about 1960, when it was developed as a petrol filling station.

The Bell Inn, Dudley Port, 1932. The licensee at this time was Jane Willis. The fence on the left encloses the pub's bowling green and the gable end in the distance belongs to the Nags Head in Groveland Road. The Bell was demolished in 1978.

Dudley Port looking towards the Old Port bridge, 1935. The cobblestones on the left indicate Groveland Road and the scaffolding beyond denotes the Alhambra Cinema under construction. The tram lines and overhead wires relate to the no. 74 route between Birmingham and Dudley, which had double track except at two points, Ryland aqueduct and Old Port bridge, because of the narrowness of the structures. On the extreme right is the fish and chip shop of John Thomas Guest, which was demolished soon after this picture was taken along with all the other houses. The business then moved to another fish and chip shop further down the road opposite the Waggon and Horses pub, which operated until 1984.

The Alhambra Cinema was officially opened on Easter Monday, 8 April 1935 by Councillor A.F. Welch, Chairman of the Urban District Council, who said that he regarded the new cinema as part of the process of beautifying that part of Tipton. The opening programme included the film *Sing As We Go*, starring Gracie Fields. Of the five cinemas within the Tipton boundary, the Alhambra was the last survivor, closing on 3 August 1963, after which the building became an electrical warehouse; it was photographed in that guise in September 1968. Demolition took place in 1989.

Birmingham Corporation tramcar no. 617 (built in 1920) heads towards Dudley, past the Waggon and Horses public house, 14 April 1938. Atkinson's, a Birmingham brewery established in 1855 and taken over by Mitchell's and Butler's in 1959, were advertising mild and bitter at 5*d* and 7*d* a pint. The pub was renamed the Melting Pot in February 1975 and closed in 1996.

Houses on the north side of Dudley Port opposite the Waggon and Horses public house, mid-1930s. The houses are not shown on the 1938 OS map, so the photograph was probably taken as an official record shortly before their clearance. The tram poles and lines can be clearly seen, but were themselves to disappear following withdrawal of the tram service on 2 April 1939.

In the days before mass motoring most large firms arranged annual outings to the seaside. In the shadow of Dudley Port railway bridge a group of Horseley Piggott employees and their families gather outside the Royal Oak before boarding a fleet of coaches for their works outing to Blackpool, 21 September 1946.

The time is 12.50 p.m. on Sunday 6 December 1964 and the 112-year-old blue-brick railway bridge at Dudley Port is blown up, watched by a large crowd of spectators from a safe distance. The first attempt at 3.20 a.m. was unsuccessful as it only dislodged one brick, and so the size of the charge had to be increased. The bridge was being reconstructed in preparation for the electrification of the railway line and to enable the road beneath to be widened into a dual carriageway.

Dudley Port station viewed from the temporary footbridge looking towards Birmingham, 1964. This footbridge was built to give access to a temporary platform which served Wolverhampton-bound trains, while the original platform was being demolished. The new station was built on the site of the old island platform in order to retain the existing subway and steps. Note the gas lighting still in use and the New Main Line canal on the right.

In the early hours of 9 September 1899 the bank of the New Main Line canal collapsed into the marlhole of the Rattlechain brickworks and over 6 miles of canal drained into the breach. This view looking towards Dudley Port shows the dry bed of the canal with wrecked boats and the damage caused to the adjacent embankment of the Stour Valley railway. The brickworks were to blame for digging clay too near to the canal.

A Birmingham (Snow Hill) to Dudley train passes through Dudley Port low-level station behind an ex-Great Western Prairie tank loco No. 4146, 25 July 1959. Passenger services ceased in July 1964 and the railway closed completely in March 1993, but the track remains in place pending a possible reintroduction of passenger trains between Stourbridge and Walsall.

Dudley Port viewed from the railway embankment, *c.* 1935. The shops featured are Jonas Booth, newsagent and confectioner; Mrs Ellen Archer, shopkeeper; Mrs Sarah Pearson, fried-fish dealer and Hipkins Bros, painters. To the right can be seen the large structure of St Paul's Methodist Chapel. The sign on the milk cart urges 'use and drink Hardings milk', this being the business of Ernest Harding of Dartmouth Street, West Bromwich.

St Paul's Methodist Chapel in Dudley Port was built in 1836 and enlarged in 1875, when the twin towers were added. In 1867 the Sunday school had 395 children on its books and 53 teachers. The chapel closed in 1966 following the discovery of serious structural problems. The Sunday school is seen here celebrating its anniversary in 1935.

A class at Dudley Port School, c. 1932. On the left is the headmaster Mr Allen and at the rear is the teacher Mr Langford, who later became headmaster at Park Lane School. Dudley Port School was opened by the Tipton Schools Board in 1875 and was closed in 1938, although the buildings were not demolished until after the Second World War.

The Vono factory and sports grounds seen from the New Main Line canal adjacent to the Ryland aqueduct, 1962. With its backdrop of the Rowley Hills, this view changed dramatically when the sports area in the foreground was developed into a private housing estate in 1991. A link with the past was maintained when the new estate roads were named after historic Tipton personalities, for example Wenyon, Peake, Bedworth and Haines.

The Dudley Dodger, 24 August 1950. From 1854 to 1964 the Dodger provided a four-minute shuttle service from Dudley to connect with most of the main-line trains which stopped at Dudley Port high level. Here the Dodger, powered by an ex-LNWR tank engine No. 46712 of 1890s vintage, awaits its next trip in the bay platform at Dudley Port. Note the boxes of Palethorpe's products on the platform.

In 1962 pleasure boats were a comparative rarity on the Black Country canals and *Water Elf II* attracts attention as it cruises past Dudley Port station. This long straight section of canal between Dudley Port and Albion was the last length of the Thomas Telford New Main Line canal to be completed, opening in 1838. The new route cut the distance between Birmingham and Wolverhampton down to 15 miles from the original 1772 line of 22½ miles. In the distance is the chimney-stack of the Rattlechain brickworks, which remained in production until the mid-1960s (see page 35).

The Dudley to Walsall diesel train is slowing as it approaches Dudley Port low-level station, 25 July 1959. Turning 90 degrees to the right from the above location reveals a panorama southwards towards Dudley with its medieval castle prominent on the skyline. In the right distance is the factory chimney of Palethorpe's factory and to the left of the railway is Palethorpe's reception siding, where pigs would arrive by rail ready to be processed into sausages and pies.

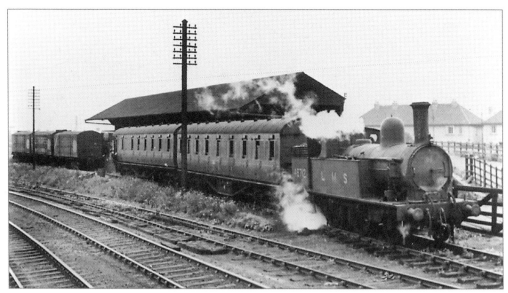

Palethorpe's private railway siding just to the west of Dudley Port station, where live pigs were delivered for slaughter and finished products dispatched in the famous red railway vans. The vans would often be collected by the Dudley Dodger in between passenger duties, as seen here in 1951, and taken either to Dudley Port high level or Dudley where they were attached to main-line trains. In the right background are the council houses of Tudor Street, built in the late 1930s. The area occupied by Palethorpe's siding was redeveloped as Tudor Court in the late 1960s.

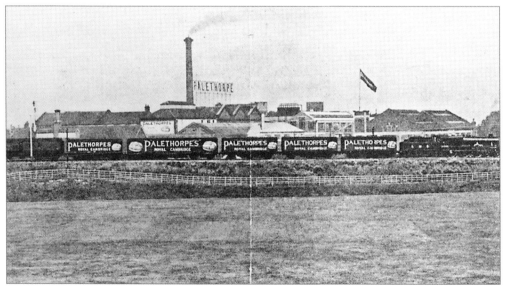

A publicity photograph entitled 'Christmas Sausage and Pie Orders 1937 – Refrigerated Vans in Daily Use'. From the 1880s to the mid-1960s Palethorpe's used their own liveried railway vans to deliver their products to all parts of the country. In 1913 the LNWR staff magazine reported that 'Comparatively few are the stations on the North Western system that do not receive each week one or more securely packed boxes whose labels indicate that they contain a consignment of the succulent breakfast fare specialised by Messrs Palethorpe.' The train has been specially posed beside the factory and photographed from across Palethorpe's sports ground.

A trade card for the Whitehouse Brothers' Model Brewery in Park Lane, illustrating their impressive range of buildings. Little is known about the company other than that George and Elisha Whitehouse were brewing by 1865 and that they had ceased by 1886, as the OS map of that year shows the brewery as 'disused'. It was obviously an ambitious enterprise at a time when most Black Country pubs produced their own 'home brewed' beer. The vacant buildings were purchased by Palethorpe's in 1890.

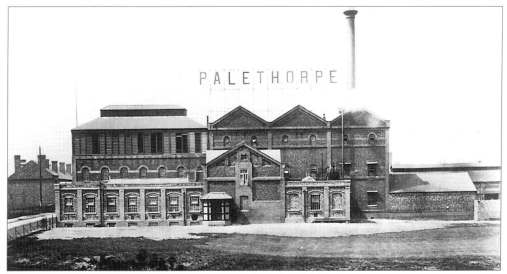

The model brewery had become a model sausage factory by the end of the nineteenth century. Palethorpe's added their name and some small extensions, but the buildings are still clearly recognizable from the brewery trade card above. The picture was taken from the railway embankment with Park Lane East in the foreground. The open ground in front of the buildings was used for the expansion of the firm and had been built on by the 1920s.

The Palethorpe's boiler house with its three Lancashire boilers, which can be seen at the right-hand end of the bottom picture on p. 41. This faced on to an area of derelict mine workings which was later reclaimed to become Victoria Park; this was officially opened in 1901. The south end of the park was dominated by Palethorpe's until its closure in 1968.

By 1900 about 100 girls were engaged in linking 'Royal Cambridge' sausages, and the firm remained a big employer of female labour right up until its closure. An account contemporary with this picture boasted that the sausages 'have been constantly supplied to Her Majesty's household at Windsor Castle and Osborne House and Mr Palethorpe's list of distinguished patrons also included HRH The Prince of Wales, HIM The Empress of Austria and numerous members of the notability.'

The small back-to-back houses in Brewery Street, which dated from about 1870, photographed shortly before their demolition, late 1960s. The street took its name from Whitehouse Brothers' Model Brewery (see page 41).

Members of the Coneygre Mission Sunday school, 1951. A mission church to St Martin's, this small brick structure, with a bell cote from which rang a single bell, was built in 1910 with one Brother Holmes in charge. Standing on the extreme right is Harold Baggott, the Sunday school superintendent. The mission closed in March 1973.

The Boscobel Tavern in Boscobel Street which took its name from the Boscobel oak in Shropshire in which Charles II is said to have hidden after the Battle of Worcester. The old building was demolished following its replacement by a new pub of the same name on the corner of Hill Street and Park Lane West, which opened on 10 March 1978. This picture, dated August 1968, shows the gap between the houses left by the recent demolition of Palethorpe's factory.

A happy group of locals line up outside the Boscobel Tavern, c. 1920. They are possibly about to embark on a charabanc outing, although the significance of the paperchain is not known. The man in the waistcoat is thought to be the landlord, William Bates. Before the Second World War the Boscobel was one of the many smaller locals which were licensed only to sell beer.

In 1952, the year that Palethorpe's celebrated their centenary, their football team won the coveted Palethorpe's Ball Trophy. Mr Henry Palethorpe had given the trophy for competition between teams in the Birmingham Works Football Association some twenty-four years earlier and this was the first time the club had won it, although they had once previously reached the final.

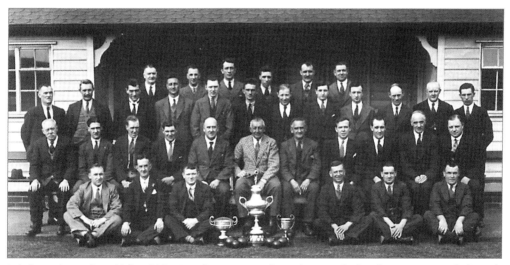

Palethorpe's Bowling Club, 1930s. Members pose with trophies on the bowling green at Palethorpe's sports ground in Sedgeley Road West. Seated in the centre of the group is Henry (Inie) Palethorpe. On the extreme right of the second row back is Sergeant Harry Rogers DCM who lost a leg in the First World War. He was such a good bowler that he had a special crutch made with an enlarged rubber pad on the bottom to protect the green from marking.

In 1936 Tipton Harriers built a new headquarters on the corner of Park Lane West and Coneygre Road opposite Palethorpe's sports ground. Here Mr Henry (Inie) Palethorpe, centre in cap, performs the opening ceremony accompanied by the Harriers' committee. On his left are Jim Partridge and Bill Patrick, the club secretary. The gentleman on the left holding his hat is Councillor W.G.W. George.

A group of cheerful Tipton Harriers outside their headquarters, c. 1960. Standing, left to right: Jack Baker, Ken Rickhouse, Jim Wright, Arthur Fellows, Pete Boxley, Bryan Thorpe, Dave Henderson, John Reniket, John Allen, Joe Gripton, Ron Bentley, Len Myerscough, Bert Harbach and Colin Anderson. Crouching at the front: Geoff Wood, Erik Silk and Terry Jones. Jack Baker (1883–1961), who helped to found the Harriers, served the club as trainer for over fifty years. He is seen in his younger days on page 107.

Joseph Atkins and his fiancée Flora Morris are about to enjoy a spin on his Raleigh 2.48 hp motorcycle outside the Park Hotel, Victoria Road, in the mid-1930s. Mills' shop in the background invited passers-by to try their deluxe ices. The Park Hotel closed in 1996 and has since been converted into flats.

Victoria Road viewed from the railway bridge, 1955. Also seen are the Central Library with its impressive tower and terracotta work, the Park Hotel with a grotesque figure over the doorway and the boundary wall of the Park Methodist chapel. The houses on the left were demolished in the late 1970s and the site is now occupied by a doctors' surgery opened in 1996. On the right is Lakin's fish and chip shop.

Tipton Harriers Cross Country team, winners of the Birmingham Cross Country League, 1950. Left to right: Harold Williamson, Brendon Twomley, Jack Corfield, Len Myerscough, Stan Dean (no. 223, wearing an army running vest and who was serving with the REME), Don Osbourne, -?-, Arthur Fellows, Arthur Cole (English international), Tim Bedford, Dave Hardisty.

Members of the Hall family pose for a photograph outside Henry Hall's butcher's shop in Park Lane East with the 1938 Christmas fayre display. Henry Hall stands on the extreme left, while on the extreme right is Ruth Evans, his sister, who ran the florist's shop next door. The family started their butcher's business in Great Bridge in 1863 with William Hall.

The Bolt & Nut Co., Park Lane East, 1968. This photograph was taken before the offices and houses seen here were replaced by a new office block in the early 1970s. The company specialized in nuts, bolts, rivets and washers, and in the postwar era the firm's chief customers were electrical undertakings, constructional engineers and rolling-stock repairers. A BR class 47 diesel loco passes on the Stour Valley line in the distance, while just below two cars negotiate the narrow arch of the Puppy Green canal aqueduct.

Park Lane East from the Puppy Green aqueduct, 1968. Seen in the picture are the 'twenty-four steppins' up to the canal towpath, the Bolt & Nut works and the Wellington public house. The old cottages on the right were demolished in the 1970s. The local name Puppy Green had fallen into disuse by the end of the nineteenth century, but was revived in 1995 at the suggestion of the Tipton Civic Society in the form of a new street name nearby.

Men at the Mond gasworks, *c.* 1930. The Mond gasworks was established in 1901 to supply gas of a low calorific value to local industry and was quite separate from the adjacent town gasworks which supplied domestic consumers. Front row, left to right: J. Gough, W. Walton, A. Edwards, J. Brothwood, W. Williams (Manager), F. Wardle (Assistant Engineer) J. Elwell, J. Jones, H. Johnson. Back row: F. Bamford, L. Roberts, J. Marsh, S. Elwell, H. Hartland, B. Humphries, J. Wilkinson, J. Rollason, J. McDabb, F. Gee, J. Whitehouse. J. Hemmings, J. Mansell. Around the valve wheel: J. Jones, L. Boothe, L. Swann.

A 'Britannia' class loco No. 70047 passes the Mond Gasworks with the daily Glasgow to Birmingham express, 5 March 1960. The train was about to stop at Dudley Port as did many of the long distance express services until the mid-1960s. On the left can be seen the New Main Line canal with the photographer standing on the bridge which took the railway over the Dixons branch canal.

GREAT BRIDGE
& HORSELEY HEATH

Great Bridge market-place was dominated by the Limerick public house, whose bar ran the whole length of the building and faced on to the small triangular blue-brick open market-place. The sign above the door advertises the 1955 horse show and gymkhana. The bridge in the background bearing the name of Ratcliff & Co. Ltd, local manufacturers of brass and copper strips, carried the GWR line between Great Bridge and Swan Village. The line was opened in 1866, and had closed to passengers by 1964 and to goods traffic by 1968.

Great Bridge Wesleyan Church was founded by an ardent band of Wesleyans who met together in Horseley Heath in about 1800. The first church on the site was created in 1811 but was superseded by this new building in 1840, when the resident minister was Nehemiah Cumock; he subsequently became the editor of the *Methodist Recorder*. The church, demolished in the 1970s, contained a memorial window to William Bedworth, the Great Bridge grocer and one-time Chairman of the Tipton School Board who died in 1898.

A Midland Red Guy bus on the no. 244 Wednesbury to Cradley Heath service turns into Market Street, Great Bridge, behind the Limerick pub, early 1960s. On the right is Joseph Wiltshire's pawnbroker's shop complete with traditional sign. The front porch and parapet of Great Bridge Wesleyan church are just visible.

People wait for the no. 244 bus to Wednesbury at the Midland Red bus stop in Market Street, August 1968. Market Street had been Limerick Passage until widening took place in about 1910, when the buildings on the right were constructed. They in turn were swept away in the late 1980s for the new traffic island which formed the first phase of the Great Bridge bypass and link to the Black Country New Road. On the left is the rear of the Limerick and in the distance the Nags Head, both of which have survived redevelopment in recent years.

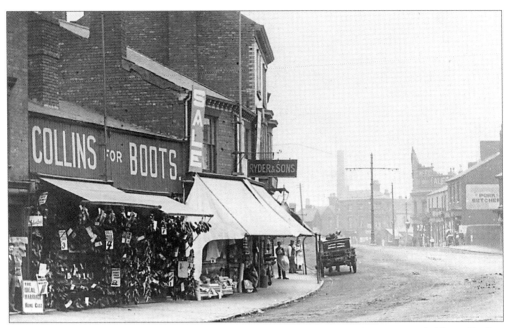

Great Bridge market-place with a horse-drawn Tipton UDC dustcart parked in remarkably traffic-free surroundings, *c*. 1910. The shoe shop of Alfred Collins is holding a huge sale while Ryders and Sons have pulled down their ample blinds to protect their delicate drapery and hosiery from the sun. In the right distance is the brick parapet of the canal bridge and beyond that the Stork Hotel, with some very prominent roof-level advertising.

A West Bromwich Corporation bus dating from 1948 stands on the bridge over the Haines branch canal at Great Bridge, 1962. It appears to be a no. 74 service to Birmingham, although the destination blind and the route indicator are inconclusive. The cottages on the left were built by the Birmingham Canal Navigations to house canal workers and survived until the late 1970s.

A Birmingham Corporation tramcar unloads in Great Bridge, having terminated a no. 76 short working of the no. 74 route from Birmingham, 9 August 1938. Horse-drawn trams from Birmingham reached Great Bridge and Dudley Port as early as 1873 and the service converted to steam and extended to Burnt Tree and Dudley in 1885. Electrification took place in 1903. Trams were withdrawn on 2 April 1939 when the route was taken over by a bus service jointly operated by West Bromwich and Birmingham Corporations.

The girls of Standard III at Great Bridge School, 1927–8. The number of children on the school register at that time was 340 boys, 317 girls and 233 infants. This was the first school to be built by the Tipton School Board and was opened in 1874. Today the school is still housed in the original buildings, thus being the last vestige of the Board schools to remain in Tipton.

A former GWR diesel railcar enters Great Bridge South station with a Dudley to Birmingham Snow Hill service, 13 April 1957. The station was opened by the GWR in 1866 as part of the 1½ mile link between its Birmingham to Wolverhampton main line at Swan Village and the LNWR Dudley to Walsall line at Great Bridge, in order to allow through running of services from Dudley to Birmingham. Passenger trains were withdrawn in June 1964. In the background are the works of Horseley Bridge and Thomas Piggott, who were no doubt responsible for the steel pipes awaiting dispatch in the adjacent goods yard. The station site and line to Swan Village have now been obliterated by the construction of the Great Bridge bypass and Black Country New Road.

A horse-drawn day boat, complete with coke brazier on the back, passes through the bottom lock of the Ryders Green flight, 1965. The boundary between Tipton and West Bromwich ran along the River Tame which passed beneath the canal just beyond the lock, the parapet of the aqueduct being visible just above the boat. The railway bridge in the background carried the Great Bridge to Swan Village railway line which closed to all goods traffic in December 1967. This route is now occupied by the Great Bridge bypass, which has been named Great Western Way.

Willow Wren boats at the wharf of Tailby and Cox timber merchants on the Haines branch canal at Great Bridge with Tame Road bridge in the background, 1965. Imported timber was brought up the River Thames in barges to Brentford and there transhipped to narrow boats for conveyance to the Midlands. The journey from Brentford to Great Bridge took five and a half days.

The crew of the narrow boats *Cygnus* and *Coleshill* moored at the Tailby and Cox wharf carry out chores while the baby in the pushchair looks on. The Willow Wren Canal Carrying Company was formed in 1953 in an attempt to reverse the decline in canal carrying, but despite some success, mainly on the Grand Union canal, the firm ceased trading in 1970. The timber traffic to Great Bridge finished in 1966.

In the early 1960s a Walsall to Dudley diesel train passes Horseley Fields junction where the Great Western branch to Birmingham Snow Hill via Swan Village and West Bromwich joined the South Staffordshire line. The photograph is taken from beneath the bridge carrying Horseley Road over the railway and shows the works of Horseley Bridge and Thomas Piggott on the left, while to the right is the Durham Ox public house in Railway Street.

A birthday celebration in progress at the Seven Stars Inn, Tame Road, in the mid-1960s. On the right is Jim Monahan, often the instigator of such parties, who was better known by his adopted name of Charlie Blackout. This resulted from his wartime reputation for painting blackouts on the roof glazing of local factories, and the subsequent naming of his maintenance business 'Blackout of Tipton'.

Workers at G.H. Whitehouse and Son Ltd, 1930s. The firm designed and built special-purpose machine tools and equipment and their premises were located on the north side of Horseley Heath between Doughty Street and Scott Street.

A large pipework fabrication leaves the Atlas works of Horseley Bridge & Thomas Piggott Ltd on a low loader, late 1950s. The Atlas works specialized in tube manufacturing and was isolated from the main Horseley Piggott site by the South Staffordshire railway, the access being from Scott Street, a short cul-de-sac off Horseley Heath. The shop in the corner is Jukes the grocer.

An early Leyland Cub, belonging to Stanton's, with the coachwork built by Samuel Holbrook of Wolverhampton. It is seen just before delivery outside Holbrook's works in Park Lane, Wolverhampton, with the Paget Arms in the background. Stanton Brothers started in business before the First World War selling coal from a horse and cart. They purchased their first motor lorry in 1925 followed by their first coach in 1931. Their cream and blue, then later red and blue, coaches were a familiar sight around the Horseley Heath garage until they were sold to Kendrick's of Princes End in 1955, although the haulage business continued until 1975.

The triangular piece of land at the junction of Horseley Heath Lower Church Lane and Park Lane East used to be known as 'The Fountain' because of the presence of a stone fountain, complete with gas lamp, seen here in about 1905. It was placed there in 1889 by the Tipton Local Board of Health at a cost of £150, but disappeared long before the Second World War, only to be replaced by an ugly brick and concrete air-raid shelter when war broke out. The area behind the small shop on the left was later to became the garage for Stanton's lorries and coaches. The white façade to the left of the three-storey block belongs to Horseley Tavern.

As people wait at a temporary bus stop at 'The Fountain' in the late 1960s, the Horseley Tavern and other buildings on the opposite side of Horseley Heath are still recognizable from the earlier Edwardian view. Most of the older buildings beyond the Horseley Tavern have been demolished and the pub itself was extensively modernized in the 1980s, although it still retains an unspoilt appearance from the outside.

In the late 1920s Leedham's second-hand furniture shop occupied 2 Horseley Heath, part of a fairly grand three-storey block which turned the corner from the main road on to the western side of 'The Fountain' triangle. The everyday furniture and domestic artefacts on sale here would probably be considered quite collectable seventy years on. The range of buildings was demolished in the early 1960s.

The Dixons branch canal, viewed from Lower Church Lane, 1970. This canal was opened in 1828 and ran for a length of ¾ of a mile to serve the new site of the Horseley Iron and Coal Company. It was named after Edward Dixon, one of the proprietors of the firm. The canal closed in 1965, but remained in a derelict condition for many years.

The Britannia, Lower Church Lane, 1969. This pub was typical of many small pubs which started life as terraced houses; its front extension incorporates a pair of characterful bay windows. The adjacent houses were demolished in the early 1970s and the pub was renamed the Black Countryman on 19 December 1975, following a request by locals after the completion of a refurbishment scheme. The inn sign now depicts a Black Country iron worker, although the figure of Britannia in the etched glass window still survives.

The new parish church of St Martin's, 1837. The surroundings appear largely rural with grazing sheep, but industry has invaded the scene, with a colliery engine house on the right and a smoking chimney-stack in the distance. The Mond gasworks were to occupy the site to the south of the church (on the right) from 1901.

Children in a classroom at St Martin's School, Lower Church Lane with their teacher Mrs Groves, c. 1931. The wooden box on the front desk bears the wording 'Mild Woodbine Cigarettes', no doubt a cast-off from a local shop and used for carrying a pupil's pens and pencils.

A memorial window in St Martin's Church to the Revd Wilson Thomas De Vine who was the Vicar of Tipton from 1895 to 1921. The stained glass window depicts St Martin sharing his cloak with a beggar. In the background is a scene contemporary with the design of the window showing Lower Church Lane, with St Martin's Church and the adjacent gasworks. Are there any other church windows which feature a gasworks?

The members of St Martin's School football team, 1938. Long before the 1870 Elementary Education Act required local elected School Boards to build schools funded from the rates, the Church of England had from 1811 begun to provide National Schools for 'Promoting the education of the poor'. Tipton had six National Schools, one of which was St Martin's which opened in 1862 and is now the oldest school building still in use in the town.

The rear of 63 Lower Church Lane with, from left, John Winterborn, his grandson Douglas, son Albert Edward and friend, with Hale's foundry forming the backdrop, mid-1930s. John Winterborn was an agent for the Birmingham Canal Navigation and Albert Edward worked for Horseley Piggott; he was involved with the erection of the Dome of Discovery at the Festival of Britain in 1951. Grandson Douglas eventually lectured in law at Wulfrun College, Wolverhampton, until his retirement in the early 1990s.

Carrier's fish and chip shop at 61c Lower Church Lane, 1930s. The business was owned by Wilfred Oscar Carrier and was situated opposite St Martin's Church, but closed in 1937. The building survived until the 1960s.

Iron moulders at Hale's Foundry take a well-earned breather while the photographer records their working environment, 1930s. The company was established in 1909 in Walsall by brothers Wilfred Edgar Hale and Thomas Leo Hale, moving to the Lower Church Lane site at Tipton in 1917 where their premises eventually grew to cover an area of over 16 acres. Their products included castings for the agricultural, electricity, railway, automotive, mining and ship-building industries made from their 'Blackheart' malleable iron.

The Court House, Lower Church Lane, late 1960s. The pub was so named because it was built opposite Tipton police station, which housed the town's magistrates' court until 1966 when local government reorganization transferred the facility to West Bromwich. Hale's Foundry, whose entrance gates can just be seen to the left of the pub, was still a major employer at this time.

The Little Burton Inn with the gasworks behind, May 1969. Alexandra Road was originally Workhouse Lane, but was renamed during the reign of Edward VII in honour of his wife, Queen Alexandra. The pub closed in the late 1980s and has now been converted to residential use, and the site of the gasworks has been reclaimed for housing development since 1991.

The old Tipton workhouse, thought to date from the sixteenth century, which stood at the corner of Lower Church Lane and Workhouse Lane (now Alexandra Road). Local government in Tipton started here on 10 September 1855 when the Local Board of Health held its first meeting in an upper room in the building. This picture is thought to have been taken just before the demolition of the workhouse in September 1912.

The site of the workhouse can be pinpointed by the advertisement hoardings on the right of this May 1969 photograph which is dominated by the new gas plant. This was described as the most modern of its kind in Europe when it opened in 1967, but owing to the emergence of North Sea gas it had a very short life. This view is taken from a spot adjacent to the grammar school (now the Alexandra High School) across the pit banks which were once very much part of the Tipton landscape but have now virtually disappeared with the reclamation schemes of recent decades.

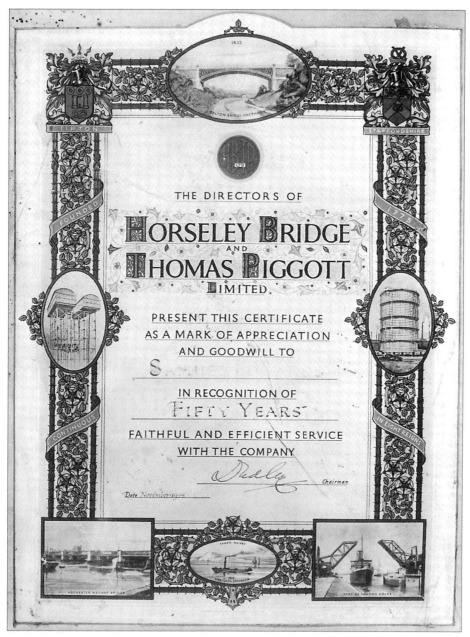

A Horseley Piggott long-service certificate presented to Samuel Edwards in 1945. The Horseley Company was one of Tipton's largest and best-known firms. Established in about 1770 as the Horseley Iron and Coal Co., the firm became famous in the early nineteenth century for its structural ironwork and large-scale engineering products. In 1822 it produced the world's first iron steamship, the *Aaron Manby*, and in 1829 the Galton Bridge, Smethwick, designed by Thomas Telford and at that time one of the world's largest single-span cast-iron bridges. Both of these achievements together with other typical products are illustrated around the edge of the certificate. In more recent times Horseley Bridge and Thomas Piggott Ltd, as it became in 1933, produced the Dome of Discovery, the huge aluminium structure which graced the Festival of Britain in 1951. After a succession of take-overs in the 1970s and '80s the works closed in 1992.

The Shrubbery public house, Horseley Road, 1937. This pub was named after a shrubbery which once lined the approach road to the nearby Amphletts Hall. A new pub of the same name was opened on 10 March 1939 a short distance away at the junction with Alexandra Road. Note the Midland Red bus timetable to the left of the doorway which probably gives details of the 244 Dudley to Wednesbury service that commenced in 1930.

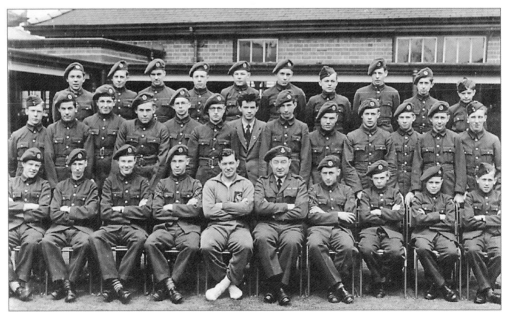

Members of the Tipton Grammar School Air Training Corps in the school quadrangle, early 1950s. In the centre of the front row are PE master Mr Hemmings and woodwork teacher Mr G. Paxton.

OCKER HILL & TOLL END

Aerial view of Ocker Hill power station, 1976. This site was established in 1899 by the Midland Electricity Corporation for Power Distribution and was described at the time as 'the largest electric power installation in England'. The coal-fired station can be seen near the end of its working life with the new oil-fired plant under construction. This new station is a fully automated peak-load generator which can be started quickly to respond to periods of high demand. The Black Country New Road, which opened in 1995, now sweeps through the space between the old and new station sites.

Coal deliveries to the power station, 1951. From its opening coal was supplied to the power station from local collieries by narrow boat on the adjacent Walsall canal, but in 1946 railway sidings were installed in readiness to serve new larger generators commissioned in 1948. However, coal continued to be delivered by canal until September 1960 and here the travelling grab cranes can be seen unloading boats with the railway sidings in the background.

A close up of one of the coal grabs which had to be manually filled from the boats before depositing the coal on to conveyors, for transportation to the bunkers on the opposite side of the canal. At its peak output in the late 1960s the station was consuming 2,000 tons of coal per day. With a narrow boat holding just 20 tons and the labour-intensive method of working it is not difficult to see why canal carrying lost out to the railways. The wooden cooling towers in the background were made redundant with the building of a new concrete cooling tower in 1956.

Ocker Hill Road, August 1968. This road, under the shadow of the cooling towers, formed part of the old main road from Great Bridge to Bilston until the construction of the shorter Gospel Oak Road in the mid-nineteenth century. The houses on the right were demolished in the mid-1970s and the site redeveloped with three-storey housing association flats.

With the end of commercial traffic on the canals, boat graveyards became a common sight throughout the Black Country. This former coal wharf on the Walsall canal at Leabrook, seen here in 1968, contains abandoned boats that could well be the ones seen delivering coal to Ocker Hill power station in the previous photographs. The houses are located in Bannister Street, named after Arthur Edward Bannister who served on Tipton UDC from 1913 to 1938 and held the position of Chairman in 1931. Looming above the houses are chimneys of the Patent Shaft steelworks in neighbouring Wednesbury.

The Bush public house, Leabrook Road, August 1968. This pub is positioned tight up against the bridge over the Walsall canal. The Ocker Hill cooling towers dominated the landscape in this area until their demolition on the morning of Sunday 18 August 1985. The power station site has since been reclaimed for housing development.

The view from Ocker Hill down the A461 Leabrook Road towards Wednesbury, September 1968. Most of the houses and shops seen here were demolished in the 1970s. The Lea Brook, at the bottom of the dip, formed the boundary between Tipton and Wednesbury and at 398 feet above sea level is Tipton's lowest point. The Dudley–Walsall road was renumbered the A4037 in November 1995 with the opening of the Black Country New Road, which relieved Leabrook Road of much of its through traffic.

The Railway Tavern at the top of Leabrook Road, 1968. The pub took its name from the Princes End branch railway which passed beneath the road at Ocker Hill island and was one of many in the Black Country owned by Atkinson's Brewery of Aston, Birmingham. It was closed and demolished with the adjacent houses in 1978.

Spring Street, Ocker Hill, 1968. Beneath this spot ran the culvert through which canal water was pumped from the Walsall level up to the Wolverhampton level in order to maintain a sufficient volume of water in the higher canals. Steam pumps at the BCN workshops (situated a few yards behind the photographer) operated from 1785 to 1948. The wall on the right was that of St Mark's Church of England School. The houses on the left were demolished in the mid-1970s.

The view down Toll End Road from Ocker Hill island, August 1968. The Cottage Spring public house, demolished in 1977, is seen on the right. This was one of three pubs in Tipton with that name, probably derived from a spring that issued nearby before the area became built up.

Gospel Oak Road, September 1968. This road was built in the mid-nineteenth century to cut short the distance between Ocker Hill and Gospel Oak; it was still referred to as New Road on the 1902 OS map. It carried the Wednesbury to Dudley tram line, which opened in 1885. The route was operated by steam trams until its closure in 1904 owing to mining subsidence. It reopened in 1907 with electric trams, but these were replaced by Midland Red buses in 1930.

The Royal Exchange, Gospel Oak Road, 1968. The pub was better known as 'Goughies' after Leonard Gough, the long-standing landlord, who held the licence from the 1920s to the 1960s. The pub closed in 1994 and was demolished a year later. The cottages adjoining disappeared in about 1976.

Workmen of the firm of Martin and Element, slag dealers, pose cheerfully at their Gospel Oak works, *c.* 1930. They were engaged in reclaiming discarded blast-furnace slag for use in road building on the land bounded by Wednesbury Oak and Gospel Oak Roads and now occupied by Tipton Sports Union. In the first half of the nineteenth century this area was the site of Gospel Oak ironworks, which in 1843 supplied the iron columns and beams for the Albert Dock in Liverpool.

Over forty years later on the same site HRH the Duke of Edinburgh meets veteran Tipton Harrier Jack Holden at the opening of the Tipton Sports Union, Gospel Oak Road, 4 June 1971. Looking on is Mr L.W. Stevenson JP, Chairman of the Sports Union (left), and Mr George Price, the then President of the Tipton Harriers (right). The date 1950 on Jack Holden's vest denotes the year of his most distinguished European and Commonwealth victories. The Gospel Oak tavern can be seen over the Duke's right shoulder.

Joshua Churchman, Mayor of West Bromwich, presents a cheque at the Gospel Oak Tavern (Mother Shipton's), 1966. He is accompanied by his wife, Mayoress Violet Churchman. Councillor Churchman served on Tipton Borough Council from 1951 and would have become Mayor of Tipton in 1966 if local government reorganization had not taken place. He did, however, become the first Mayor of the enlarged West Bromwich County Borough and was a member of the new authority until 1973.

Jubilee Park, 1955. This park was officially opened on 13 April 1935 by Councillor A.F. Welch, Chairman of Tipton UDC. Covering 25 acres, it had been constructed as an unemployment relief scheme and was named to commemorate the Silver Jubilee of King George V. In the distance can be seen the line of the Ocker Hill branch canal, which was cleared in the early 1960s to make way for the Glebefields housing development.

Powis Avenue looking towards the cooling towers of Ocker Hill power station, 1968. On the left, beyond the shop, is the main entrance to Jubilee Park. To the right is Cotterills Road, which took its name from an old farm house which stood there. Powis Avenue perpetuates the name of William Henry Powis JP, a stalwart figure in Tipton's local-government history, who became Mayor in 1940.

A charity presentation at the Harrier public house, 14 December 1966. Local MP Peter Archer (now Lord Archer) is presenting a cheque as Joshua Churchman, the Mayor of West Bromwich, looks on. The Harrier took its name from the local Tipton Harriers Club; its sign originally showed an athlete on one side and a harrier bird on the other.

Employees of Tan Sad Ltd gather at The Pound, Toll End for their annual works outing to Blackpool, *c.* 1947. The election posters on the wall behind urge voters to support William Henry Powis, John William Walters and William Horace Hirons, all three of whom achieved the office of Mayor at some time.

More Tan Sad workers and their families congregate outside the factory in Toll End Road waiting to board the fleet of Don Everall's coaches. At least twelve vehicles were required to accommodate the large number of people. Opposite can be seen the old MEB offices.

Toll End Road, 1955. The Tan Sad works, famous from the 1930s to the 1960s for their baby carriages and toys, is seen on the left. On the other side of the road are the old MEB offices, which were replaced by a modern block in 1965. In the distance is the Old Crown public house.

A close up of the Old Crown when it was owned by Frederick Smith's brewery of Aston, Birmingham, in the early 1950s. Smith's were taken over by William Butler of Wolverhampton in 1955 who in turn were subsumed into Mitchell's and Butler's of Smethwick in 1960, and it was in this latter guise that the pub lived out its final years. Dating from about 1900, the Old Crown probably had the grandest façade of any Tipton pub, yet its location had no special prestige. It closed in about 1990, but the building survives, having been converted to industrial use.

A group of parents and children in their best clothes are about to set off on a Sunday school outing in an open boat on the Toll End Communication canal near Brookhouse bridge, which carried Toll End Road over the canal just out of the picture to the right. They are probably from the Aston Street Methodist Chapel, which is the last but one building on the right. In the background the buildings of New Road rise up to a point near Deris's abattoir and then drop down to the centre of Great Bridge on the left.

Naylors Garage, Bridge Road, Toll End, *c.* 1935. The building later became part of the Tan Sad works and, although much altered, still exists as a car showroom. The proprietor, Abraham Naylor, became a local councillor in 1935 and was a charter member of the Tipton Borough Council in 1938.

Lock no. 7 on the Toll End Communication canal, Boxing Day 1965. The waterway was still just about navigable at this time. Complete closure took place in 1967 and its destruction must rank as Tipton's biggest lost opportunity now that canals are considered an environmental asset. Bridge Road crosses the canal just beyond the lock on what was officially known to the canal company as Toll End bridge. The building on the extreme right is the former Moulders Arms pub.

Early nineteenth-century houses in Bridge Street photographed shortly before their demolition as part of the council's slum-clearance programme, mid-1930s. The houses, which backed on to the canal, were known locally as Boatman's Row as several were occupied by canal boatman engaged in the local short haul 'day boat' traffic. In the distance the road curves to the left to cross Toll End bridge, as seen in the preceding and following photographs.

Bridge Street after the infilling of the canal under Toll End bridge with the ever-present Ocker Hill cooling towers in the background, 1968. The derelict building on the right was originally the Moulders Arms pub, which closed in about 1913 and was converted into a shop; in more recent times this housed the drapery business of Mary Florence Davies. Behind the old pub stands the modern office block of the Midland Electricity Board, completed in 1965.

Opposite Boatman's Row on the corner of Bridge Road and Aston Street stood these early nineteenth-century cottages. They survived into the 1950s when the site was redeveloped for three-storey council flats, the boundary wall of which is visible on the extreme right of the picture above.

The dairy of J.D. Humphries in Toll End Road, March 1965. This dairy had its origins in Princes End in the 1890s, but was established at the site seen here by 1933, where pasteurized milk ('Tay' milk) was produced until 1968. Milk arrived in churns from the Stafford area and was filtered, pasteurized, homogenized, cooled and bottled on the premises before being delivered within a 3 mile radius.

A street party celebrates the coronation of King George VI in Nock Street, Toll End, 1937. The street became noteworthy as the birthplace of Joseph Davies (1889–1976) the only Tipton-born holder of the Victoria Cross, awarded for his action on the Somme in 1916. The terraced houses grouped around Nock Street, Holland Street and Moseley Street were replaced by council flats in the early 1960s.

TIPTON GREEN

Tipton Green canal junction, where the Tipton Green Locks and Toll End Communication canal, seen under the bridge, joined the Old Main Line canal by the Beehive pub, 1962. A Mitchard's coal boat seems to be turning in this wide section of canal in order to reverse into its home wharf on the other side of Owen Street bridge. The Tipton Green Locks branch was opened in 1805 but officially abandoned in 1960, the route being redeveloped as a public walkway in the 1970s and one of the lock chambers being preserved. A unique cast-iron toll house at the top lock disappeared before the Second World War and the Beehive closed in 1978.

An Edwardian boatman and his family with their narrow boat and horse on the Old Main Line canal towpath wall at Factory Road. The boat belonged to the Shropshire Union Canal Co. and the family's temporary respite could be because the company had an agent in nearby Owen Street from whom they might have received instructions. The photograph was issued as one in a series of commercial postcards depicting Black Country life by John Price and Sons of Bilston.

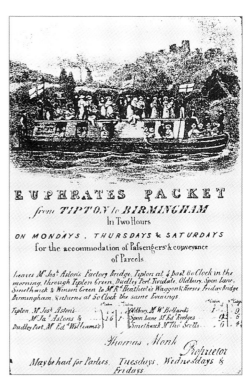

A bill poster advertising the *Euphrates* packet, a canal boat which covered the journey from Tipton to Birmingham in two hours. The *Euphrates* was a passenger 'fly-boat', of lighter build with a long wedge-like front which cut easily through the water. These were towed by horses which were maintained at an unbroken trot and changed at regular intervals. It was constructed in about 1820 by Thomas Monk at his boat dock on the Old Main Line canal near Dudley Road and this is probably the location of the illustration with Dudley Castle forming the backdrop. The boat left Factory bridge at 8.15 a.m. and returned at 5 p.m. three days a week until 1852 when the opening of the Stour Valley rendered it obsolete.

A group of locals standing outside the Three Furnaces Inn, Furnace Parade, *c.* 1925. This public house stood at the corner of Furnace Parade and Wood Street, and took its name from the three blast furnaces of the Tipton Green ironworks on the opposite side of the canal. The furnaces, a dominant feature of the skyline, were built in 1809 and worked until 1924. The pub was listed in an 1851 directory as the 'Three Furnaces and Swift Packet Office', a reference to the *Euphrates* packet boat.

A view down Owen Street as it appeared on a commercial postcard, *c.* 1900. On the left is the Fountain Inn, famous for its role as the headquarters from 1835 to 1851 of the champion prize-fighter William Perry, who, better known by his nickname of 'the Tipton Slasher', was champion of England from 1850 to 1857. The Fountain Inn has survived, despite losing its top storey in the early 1950s, and became a listed building in 1982 owing to its historical association.

A commemorative plaque was presented to the Fountain Inn by the Black Country Society to mark the pub's association with William Perry on 2 March 1984. This photograph shows John Brimble (right), President of the Black Country Society, handing over the plaque to Andrew Johnson, General Manager of the Holt, Plant and Deakin Brewery, while the 'Tipton Slasher' looks on behind.

The top end of Owen Street with the Co-op store on the right, mid-1940s. The Tipton Co-operative Society monogram indicates that the date is 1948 or earlier, as that was the year the Tipton Co-op became the Coseley and Tipton Co-op. In 1951 it merged with the Wolverhampton Co-op.

The Regal Cinema, 1955. The original cinema building in Owen Street started life as a market hall, which was converted to the Tivoli and started showing films in 1910. It was rebuilt in 1920 as the Regent and after further improvements in 1954 its name was changed to the Regal. It then survived for another six years, the last film being shown on 3 December 1960. One of the films on offer in this view is *One Good Turn*, starring Norman Wisdom.

Edgar and Alice Maud Hawkins with two of their children, Dorothy and Selwyn, standing outside their premises at 26 Owen Street, *c.* 1905. Mr Hawkins ran a bakery and confectionery business there together with dining rooms. He was a member of the Tipton Urban District Council for a short period until his death in 1914. The shop traded as Maypole's in more recent times.

The lower part of Owen Street was, and still is, dominated by St Paul's Church, built in 1837–8 and designed by the architect Robert Ebbles. When St Martin's was made redundant in the late 1980s the parishes were combined and the church became officially known as St Martin's and St Paul's. On one of the gate piers was a bench mark (height above sea level 464.26 ft). Also to be seen in this 1955 picture are Lister's hardware shop, founded by James Lister in 1874, and the office of the local newspaper, the *Tipton Herald*.

St Paul's Church viewed from the opposite direction to the previous picture, 1955. The church is flanked by Barclays Bank with its ornate cast-iron railings which, despite surviving the war, did not last into the 1960s. The bank closed in the 1980s, but the attractive gothic building survives as a betting shop. On the far side of the church the white interwar building, which housed Clarke's electrical shop at that time, was demolished in 1995 and the site laid out as a landscaped open space.

By the late 1960s Owen Street was in decline and had started to take on a forlorn appearance, as seen in this view from the bottom of the eastern end of the street, 1969. The Albion Inn on the left was one of five pubs in the street which, with one exception (the Fountain Inn, see page 90), were closed and demolished in the late 1970s redevelopment of the area. The only feature in this picture which has survived is the postbox on the corner of Albion Street.

Tipton Owen Street railway station viewed from the signal box with a Birmingham-bound express passing through hauled by 'Royal Scot' class No. 46151 *The Royal Horse Guardsman*, 1950s. The suffix 'Owen Street' was added to the station name in 1950 by British Railways to distinguish it from the former GWR station (see page 113) which was named Tipton Five Ways. The latter closed in 1962 and Owen Street station officially reverted back to plain Tipton in 1968.

Owen Street station showing the curious curved roofed buildings on the Birmingham platform together with the level crossing and the signal box which provided the vantage point for the photograph above, 1964. The Birmingham to Wolverhampton railway is still confusingly known as the Stour Valley line, so called because the original company planned to build a branch from Smethwick to Stourport. It was opened in 1852 and electrified in 1967 as part of the London to Glasgow modernization scheme, thus ensuring Tipton's survival on the railway map of Britain.

An aerial view of the works of Lee Howl and Co., *c.* 1950. The Tipton Green Furnaces Branch canal runs beneath the wooden platforms of Owen Street station to reach the basin around which the furnaces stood. In the middle distance the Old Main Line canal, opened in 1772, snakes its way along the 473 foot contour, and beyond it lies the Tibbington housing estate.

Lee Howl and Co. was founded in 1880 by brothers Edmund and Oliver Howl and William Lee. The company specialized in submersible pumps and exported to all parts of the world until its closure in the early 1980s. This picture of one of the machine shops in about 1920 shows machine tools driven by belts from overhead line shafts in cramped conditions that would horrify modern safety officers.

Workers at Bullers Ltd, 1920s. Bullers was located in Factory Road and was founded in 1890, but had its origins in Devon in 1840 when one John Buller set up a small pottery business, moving to Hanley in 1865 and acquiring the Tipton foundry of Jobson Brothers in 1885 to form Buller Jobson. The early ceramic craft developed into the production of electrical insulators, and by the 1960s the firm was describing itself as 'Engineers and Manufacturers of Porcelain Insulators and Metalwork for Electrical Transmissions'. The work closed in the early 1990s.

Jack Holden's Gardens, 1962. These gardens were laid out on a site between Walton Street and Queens Road, previously occupied by old houses, to commemorate the marathon runner Jack Holden, Tipton Harriers's most famous member. They were officially opened on 23 July 1952 by Alderman A.E. Bolton, Mayor of Tipton. Note the huge retort house of the town gasworks in the distance.

The view up Union Street from the junction with Brown Street, July 1968. This photograph was taken just before the clearance of these houses, which dated from the 1850s. Beyond the houses is the Conservative Club and the hump-backed bridge which crossed the Tipton Green Locks branch canal. Beyond the bridge are the shops and flats built in the 1950s by the council in an early attempt to modernize the town centre.

Rose Cottage, Queens Road, August 1921. This was one of a group of four houses built at the eastern end of Queens Road in 1900 and represents a well-appointed lower middle-class house of the period in stark contrast to the majority of older dwellings in the area, such as those in Union Street in the top picture. The rear of Rose Cottage was occupied by Morris's printing works.

The Tipton Carnival procession passes the Park Lane Methodist Chapel in Park Lane West with the Red Lion pub on the right, late 1960s. The carnival was instigated in 1966 by the Tipton Community Association to revive the tradition of carnivals held before the Second World War and to succeed the annual horse show and gymkhana, which ceased when Tipton was amalgamated into West Bromwich County Borough in that year.

A dignified group of gentlemen standing on the steps outside Park Lane Wesleyan Methodist church, *c*. 1910. On the front row sporting his watch chain is Edward Henry Hipkins, son of Daniel Hipkins (see page 10), who followed the family tradition of public service and Methodist devotion.

Joseph Batson commenced dealing in animal fats in 1840 and developed into a manufacturer of specialist lubricants for rolling mills and other machinery associated with the local heavy engineering industries. The old offices and narrow entrance from Dudley Road, seen here in about 1965, were swept away with the expansion of the site in the 1970s.

Members of the Dudley Canal Tunnel Preservation Society manoeuvre a wooden narrow boat used for Dudley tunnel trips into the coal wharf adjacent to Joseph Batsons works, c. 1964. The narrow section of canal to the right was originally a stop lock to maintain the level of the Dudley canal, 6 inches above that of the Birmingham canal, the junction of which is just out of the picture. The lock was removed in 1846 when the two companies amalgamated. Batsons acquired the wharf in 1957 and extended their premises on to it. Note the wooden crane.

Batsons, early 1950s. Here 5 gallon containers of lubricating oil are being loaded on to a Smethwick registered Austin A40 pick-up, while on the left a stock of specialist lubricants is maintained on a stillage ready for use in small volumes for test purposes.

A Batsons tanker used for larger orders of oil, where the products were conveyed direct to the customer's own storage facility. This immaculate West-Bromwich registered tanker proudly proclaims the Batsons trade name of 'Tiptone' in the early 1950s. The location is thought to be near the firm's premises in Castle Street. Joseph Batsons Ltd survives today as one of Tipton's oldest-established companies.

A party held at the Tipton Labour Club, Victoria Road to mark the retirement of Dan Randle (seated right), who had worked as a gardener on Jubilee Park. Celebrities in attendance included the Rt. Hon. Arthur Henderson MP, who has his hands on the shoulders of Sidney Hall, who served as Mayor of Tipton in 1955. Looking on over Mr Henderson's left shoulder is Frank Chamberlain, Mayor in 1963.

Percy Hayes (1904–82), 1950s. Percy was a gardener on Victoria Park from 1929 until his retirement in 1969. He lived in the lodge adjacent to the Queens Road entrance and is pictured here on the park's Fordson tractor. He was well known for being the master of ceremonies at the dances held at Tipton baths.

In so many ways Tipton has changed dramatically over the past sixty years and yet much of the landscape revealed on this aerial photograph of June 1935 is instantly recognizable to younger Tiptonians. The Old Main Line canal in the foreground, Palethorpe's sports ground (now Coneygre Sports Centre), Victoria Park and in the distance the parallel routes of the Stour Valley railway and New Main Line canal all still exist. Once familiar features which have disappeared

include Palethorpe's factory (centre) and the great swathe of nineteenth-century housing around Tipton Green (top left) which was almost totally obliterated by the early 1970s. A fascinating industrial remnant visible at the top right of the picture is the group of blast furnaces which had been closed down in 1924 but were not dismantled until 1938.

Old houses and shops dating from the 1860s in Park Lane West, 1968. The smaller houses were one-up, one-down back-to-backs. The opening in the centre left of the picture leads to a 'court' around which more small houses were grouped. Such houses had been the subject of clearance schemes since the 1920s and these were some of the last to remain, being demolished in the early 1970s.

The Bush public house in Park Lane West, 1968. This pub was completely wrecked in the Zeppelin raid of 1 February 1916, when a bomb bounced off the roofs of houses opposite and exploded in the road just a few feet in front of the building causing the clock to stop at 12.20 a.m. The landlord, Thomas Taylor, and his family, although cut by flying debris, had a miraculous escape. The pub was substantially rebuilt after the war, but closed in 1995.

Members of the Tipton Corps of the St John's Ambulance Brigade at the beginning of the Second World War in the playground of Park Lane School.

The Red Lion pub, Park Lane West, early 1950s. It was one of about six Tipton pubs owned by Frederick Smith Ltd of Aston, Birmingham. The pub and the building on the left were listed in 1987, and in 1993 a plaque was erected on the pub by the Tipton Civic Society to commemorate the fact that these buildings form the last pre-Victorian remnants of the old village of Tipton Green and that the Red Lion is Tipton's oldest pub.

Waterloo Street, July 1968. On the right is the Waterloo Inn, where the Tipton Harriers met before 1936 (see opposite), and the Refuge Methodist Chapel of 1887, so called because it was established by a breakaway group from the Bell Street Primitive Methodist Chapel who 'sought refuge' elsewhere following a rift. Waterloo Street had been cleared for redevelopment by 1972. Park Lane Methodist Chapel, the rear of which can be seen in the distance, was demolished in 1975 to be replaced by a smaller modern building.

Members of the Refuge Chapel in Waterloo Street, c. 1890. Non-conformity grew rapidly in Tipton from the time that John Wesley first preached at Tipton Green in 1745, and established the first Wesleyan chapel in Staffordshire on the site of what is now Park Lane Methodist Church. By the First World War there were about thirty Non-conformist places of worship spread throughout the town.

A group of Tipton Harriers in the back yard of the Waterloo Inn, Waterloo Street, the club's original headquarters in 1930. Front row, left to right: J.W. Timmins, T. Kay, S. Paskin, J.T. Holden, J.H. Plant, E. Kay. Back row: Jack Baker (trainer), A.H. Bynion, J. Hall. The photograph is titled 'Winners of Staffordshire Cross Country Championship 1926', but dated 1930.

The marathon runner Jack Holden pictured early in his career wearing an England vest and proudly displaying a trophy and medals, 1929. In his heyday he was described as the greatest distance runner of all time.

Mrs Maria Hickinbottom standing outside her florist shop at 2 Bell Street, *c.* 1930. The shop was on the south side of Bell Street in an area cleared in the mid-1950s for the Coronation House development; it is scheduled for further redevelopment in 1997.

A class at Tipton Green School, 1938. The teacher is Mr Harry Griffiths who later moved to Tipton Grammar School where he taught science. He was also known locally as a chapel pianist and organist.

Children on the platform during the Sunday school anniversary at the Coppice Street Methodist Mission, 1949. The person sitting on the extreme right is Mr Jonah Whitehouse who was superintendent at the mission at that time and later became the last Mayor of Tipton in 1966. Coppice Street chapel (or mission as it was better known) closed in the late 1960s.

Old dwellings in Hall Street just before slum clearance, early 1930s. The poster on the wall reads 'Vote For Baker' and refers to Joseph Baker, a local shopkeeper who served on Tipton Urban District Council from 1907 to 1935.

Bell Street Methodist Chapel Sunday school anniversary, *c.* 1968. The chapel, which dated from 1823, closed in the mid-1970s at the same time as Bloomfield Chapel and their congregations transferred to the newly rebuilt Park Lane Methodist Chapel.

The Tipton and Coseley Building Society was established in 1901 and occupied these premises at 60 High Street from 1927 to 1963 when they were replaced by a new office block on the same site. The society moved to larger offices in Owen Street in 1993.

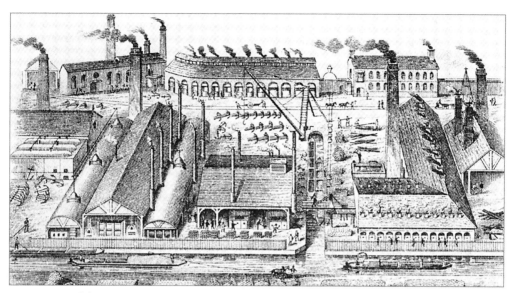

An engraving of the Neptune Forge chain and anchor works viewed from the north with the Old Main Line canal in the foreground, *c.* 1873. It was established in 1851 by Theophilus Tinsley, becoming Tinsley Wright and Co. in 1861 and Joseph Wright and Co. by 1863. It was taken over by the famous Netherton firm of Noah Hingley in 1947 and in the postwar era specialized in forging, pressure vessels, welded and heavy machined fabrications. In 1873 the firm was described thus: 'Mr Wright's chains are famous not only in London and Liverpool markets, but throughout the world; the cables made at this celebrated wharf are unrivalled.' The works were demolished in 1994 and the site is to be redeveloped in 1998 as the Neptune Health Park.

Chainmakers working on 2 inch cable or stud-link chain for maritime use at the Neptune Forge, Joseph Wright & Son, mid-1920s. The purpose of the central stud was to increase the tensile strength and to prevent the chain becoming knotted up when attached to an anchor. Cable chain was welded in the side of each link by repeated hammer blows from the chainmakers who, on larger chain, would often use a two-handled hammer or 'Johny'; an example can be seen in the foreground. From left to right the men are Bill Tibbs, an unidentified Old Hill chainmaker and Sam Paskin, who spent his spare time boxing under the stage name of Sam Brannon.

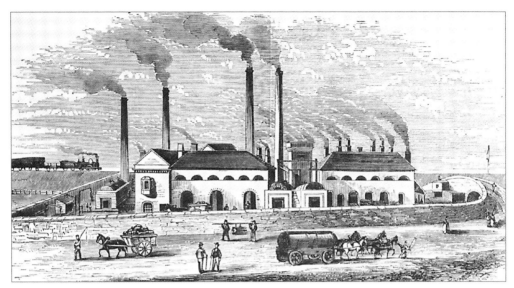

An engraving of W. Barrows and Son's factory works on the site now occupied by Beans Industries in
Hurst Lane, *c.* 1873. The railway is the GWR line between Dudley and Wolverhampton which finally
closed in 1968. Factory bridge is just out of the picture on the right. The bridge that is shown crosses a
basin branch from the Old Main Line canal serving the works and runs behind the boundary wall. On the
1884 OS map the works are shown as disused. Barrows and Son were successors to the famous Bradley,
Barrows and Hall whose BBH brand iron became renowned. The original partner, Joseph Hall, had
invented the wet puddling process which revolutionized iron making.

The chassis-erecting shop at the Hurst Lane factory of Bean Cars Ltd, with chassis for trucks on the left
and cars on the right, 1927. Completed chassis were road tested by being driven to a sister factory at
Dudley for bodies to be fitted. Car production began in 1919 and lasted until 1929, although commercial
vehicles were made until 1931. Components for the automotive industry are still manufactured in this
factory which was, until the early 1990s, still known as Beans Industries.

Great Western Railway heavy freight loco No. 3851 heads towards Dudley through Tipton Five Ways station, 8 August 1955. Passenger services between Wolverhampton, Dudley and Stourbridge on this line were withdrawn in July 1962. The tall stacks in the background belong to Beans Industries.

Sedgley Road West and the municipal buildings viewed from the end of the platform of Five Ways station, 1962. The municipal buildings were originally the offices of Bean Cars Ltd but were purchased by Tipton Urban District Council in 1934 for its new headquarters. They were officially opened on 7 March 1935 by the Rt. Hon. Arthur Greenwood MP.

Dudley Road with Five Ways in the distance and where the double tramlines provided a crossing place on the single line tramway from Wednesbury to Dudley, *c.* 1911. In the early years of operation some passengers came in for criticism as related in this contemporary account: 'Upon certain days when coursing and dog racing is going on in the vicinity of Lea Brook crowds of men literally besiege the car, several of each lot has his own dog carefully clothed in woollen, which he takes on top of the car with him, leaving a box of rabbits under the stairs. This class of passenger usually hails from Tipton Five Ways and they are found by conductors very awkward to deal with, the men naturally rough in themselves being assisted by the dogs on the slightest provocation.'

The children of Class IV with their slates at the ready at Tipton Green School, *c.* 1920. Tipton Green School was built by the Tipton School Board in 1878 and stood on the Sedgley Road West site for almost a century, until it was demolished and the school moved to its present site at Park Lane West in 1976.

CIVIC LIFE

The 1941 Mayoral group photographed in the council chamber of the municipal buildings. Left to right: Mace Bearer, Mr A.H. North; Mayoress, Mrs Bolton; Deputy Mayoress, -?-; Mayor, Alderman Arthur Bolton; Deputy Mayor, Councillor Mrs Lucy Bagnall; Town Clerk, Mr K.W. Madin. Bolton was elected to the office of Mayor on five further occasions, holding the position more times than any other member.

Members of the Tipton Urban District Council, 1938

S. DAVIS, J.P.
(Chairman of the Council).

A. F. WELCH, J.P.
(Vice-Chairman of the Council).

A. PARKER, J.P., C.C.

J. E. TOMMAS.

W. G. GIBBS.

R. A. HANCOCK.

W. A. WHITEHOUSE.

W. J. W. GEORGE.

C. W. GROVE.

F. SNEYD.

A. E. BOLTON, C.C.

J. HEMMINGS.

The members of the last Tipton Urban District Council before it was disbanded and the Tipton Municipal Borough Council was created, 1938. Of these members, Arthur Frederick Welch, William Edward Hampton, Arthur Jones and Arthur Edwin Bolton were later to hold the office of Mayor of Tipton. William Sydney Hill became General Secretary of the National Union of Public Employees and James Edmund Salter received the Freedom of the Borough. Note the male domination of the council, Mrs Lucy Bagnall being the only woman in the group and one of only six women ever to serve on Tipton Council.

Members of the Tipton Urban District Council, 1938—*continued*

W. S. HILL.

Mrs. L. BAGNALL.

W. J. RHODES.

W. E. HAMPTON.

A. JONES, C.C.

A. NAYLOR.

A. E. BANNISTER, J.P.

F. NEALE.

J. WARNER.

T. DARBY.

G. M. KENNEDY.

J. E. SALTER.

Officials
who took part in the Incorporation Inquiry on 16th December, 1936.

K. W. MADIN
Solicitor and Clerk of the Council
(Charter Town Clerk).

V. B. TRANTER
Assistant Clerk of the Council
(Deputy Charter Town Clerk).

H. N. WOODARD
Engineer and Surveyor.

R. PILLING
Treasurer.

A. HASTILOW
Director of Education.

W. WILLIAMS
Gas Engineer and Manager.

G. H. ACTON
Senior Sanitary Inspector.

H. SCRIVEN
Housing Manager.

C. R. GALLIE
Housing Director.

A. W. TAYLOR
Librarian.

The officials of the Tipton Urban District Council who took part in the Incorporation Inquiry on 16 December 1936, most of whom became household names in the small scale parochial nature of local government that existed before the impersonal larger authorities were created in the 1960s.

Officials arriving at the municipal buildings for the presentation of the Charter of Incorporation, 1 October 1938. This very important day in the history of Tipton marked the creation of the Municipal Borough of Tipton. Seen here are Mayor, Alderman A.F. Welch JP, Town Clerk K.W. Madin (in wig), the Mace Bearer, A.H. North, and the Lord Lieutenant of Staffordshire, the Earl of Harrowby, and the Countess of Harrowby.

The Mayor's civic Sunday parade passing through Great Bridge, 1938. The procession was led by the Mace Bearer, A.H. North, followed by the Mayor, Alderman A.F. Welch JP, the Deputy Mayor, Alderman W.G.W. George, and other members of the borough council.

The Tipton roll of Mayors which spans the life of the borough from 1938 to 1966, when Tipton was amalgamated with West Bromwich. This originally hung in the council chamber, but was removed and put into store in Wednesbury Art Gallery when the town lost its independence. In 1990, as a result of the campaigning by the Tipton Civic Society, it was rescued and put on permanent display in the Central Library in Victoria Road, together with a facsimile of the Grant of Arms.

The borough coat of arms which originally hung in the council chamber in the municipal buildings in Sedgley Road West. When the borough ceased to exist in 1966 it was removed to the grammar school at the instigation of the Tipton Rotary Club and Councillor Joshua Churchman, the then Mayor of the West Bromwich Borough of which Tipton had become part. In 1997 the coat of arms was moved to the Tipton Heritage Centre in Brick Kiln Street, which had been established in 1996 to collect such historic artifacts and to celebrate the achievements of Tipton's past.

John William Walters, three times Mayor of Tipton, 1958, 1959 and 1962. He was elected to Tipton Borough Council as a Labour representative in a three-cornered fight for the Ocker Hill ward. He was elected as an alderman in 1964 and served on the borough council for almost twenty years.

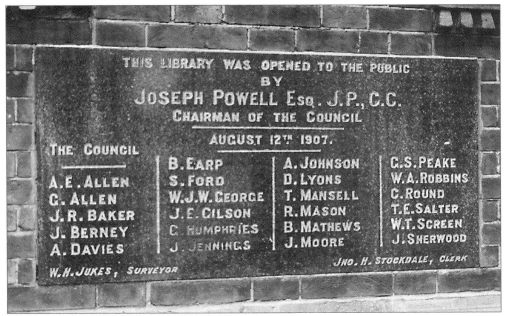

One of the foundation stones of Toll End Library, now in the care of Tipton Heritage Centre, which shows the names of the members of the Urban District Council under the chairmanship of Joseph Powell JP, and reflects the collective achievement of the town's ruling body at that time. The library closed in 1984 and, despite desperate efforts to save it, the building was demolished in 1997.

Joseph Powell (1854–1938): a leading figure in Tipton's local government in the late nineteenth and early twentieth century. He held the office of Chairman of the Urban District Council for four separate terms and in 1900 was the Chairman of the Tipton Education Committee. He was a well-known public figure and served for many years as a magistrate, was an overseer of the poor and represented the Ocker Hill division on the Staffordshire County Council. His wife, Martha, a school teacher who also took a profound interest in local affairs, was for many years a member of the Dudley Board of Guardians. Their names are perpetuated in the street name Powell Place.

Alfred Herbert North, who became the Tipton Borough Mace Bearer in 1938, pictured as a young man in the uniform of Inspector for the Birmingham and Midland Tramways. The Birmingham and Midland Tramways was a joint committee comprising representatives from four Black Country and Birmingham tramway companies, and was responsible for the day-to-day operations throughout the region from 1904.

Alfred Herbert North some years later in the uniform of the St John's Ambulance Brigade proudly showing his medals. He assisted in the creation of the Tipton branch of the brigade and was an officer for twenty-five years. He was awarded the OBE for his rescue work in the aftermath of the Zeppelin raid on Tipton in January 1916. He worked as caretaker of the public offices in Owen Street and then the municipal buildings for forty-one years and served as Mace Bearer from 1938 until his retirement in 1950.

The municipal buildings in Sedgley Road West contained the town's council chamber until 1966, when they were acquired by Dudley Technical College. They served as an annexe to the college until 1995 when they were purchased by the neighbouring firm of Newey Goodman Ltd. The hoarding on this 1955 picture advertises the forthcoming horse show and gymkhana on 16 July 1955, with the following admission prices: enclosure 2s 6d, adults 1s 6d, children 6d.

To mark the Queen's visit to Tipton in 1994, the surviving members of the old Tipton Borough Council held a reunion. Front row, left to right: Mrs Una Jones (Mayoress of Sandwell), Councillor John Padden (Mayor of Sandwell), Gwyn Williams. Back row: Cecil Walter Chater, William Woodward, Charles Baker, Joshua Churchman, Douglas Cox. The only other surviving member, Jonah Whitehouse, was ill in hospital at the time. In front of the group is the Tipton Borough mace.

The first ever visit to Tipton by a reigning monarch took place on 24 June 1994 when Queen Elizabeth spent the day visiting the Black Country, arriving at Tipton railway station by the royal train to perform her first engagement of the day at the Tipton City Challenge office in the High Street. The Queen's cavalcade is seen driving slowly along Owen Street through the massed crowds to a tumultous welcome.

Queen Elizabeth arriving at Partnership House, the headquarters of the Tipton City Challenge where she was received by Mr Colin Cooke of Triplex Industries, the Chairman of the Tipton City Challenge Board. The Queen was told of the Tipton Challenge regeneration and unveiled a plaque to mark her visit.

ACKNOWLEDGEMENTS

The authors are pleased to acknowledge the invaluable help which has been given by the following, who have loaned photographs and supplied information:

Harry Allsopp, Maurice Atkins, Mrs Atkins, Charlie Baker, Bill Bawden, Mr Betteridge, Florence Billingham, Ken Blount, Jim Boulton, Alf Breakwell, Paul Breakwell, Marion Brennan, Ray Brothwood, Andrew Bullock, Doris Bullock, Paul Bullock, Violet and Joshua Churchman, Paul Collins, John Cooksey, Jack Corfield, Gail Cox, Len Davies, John Deane, David Dugmore, Alan Doggett, Janice Endean, Hilda Francis, Iris Gaskin, Peter Glews, Joe Gripton, Michael Hale, Brian Hall, Ray Hartland, Irene Harris, Phil Hill, Stan Hill, Susan Hill, Wally Hill, Una Hodgkins, J. Hooper, Jack Hough, David Humphries, Gaynor Iddles, Mrs J. Laight, E. Lakin, Jack and Lily Lloyd, David McDougall, Michael Mensing, Mrs E. Mills, Ron Moss, Mrs Naylor, John Osborne, Mrs Paskin, Alf Perks, Fred Perks, Mrs E. Pound, Alan Price, Lucy Reed, Mr and Mrs Shelley, Thelma Smith, Mr Stacey, Jack Stanton, Bill Steventon, Ron Thomas, Mrs Torrington, Bob Trease, R. Trease, Doris Turner, Janet Turner, Mrs Warmer, Patricia Waters, Mrs Watt, Ann Watton, Vi Whetton, Barry Whitehouse, Harry Whitehouse, John Whitehouse, David Whyley, Ned Williams, Margaret Willetts, David Wilson, Douglas Winterborn, Keith Wright.

We are also grateful to:
Aerofilms Ltd, Joseph Batsons Ltd, Black Country Museum, Black Country Society, Millbrook House Ltd, National Tramway Museum, National Waterways Museum, Tipton City Challenge, Tipton Civic Society, Tipton and Coseley Building Society, Tipton Harriers, Sandwell Libraries, Sandwell Museums, William Salt Library, *Wolverhampton Express* and *Star*.

Special thanks also go to Jonathan Brimble for help in the preparation of this book.

THE BLACK COUNTRY SOCIETY

This voluntary society, affiliated to the Civic Trust, was founded in 1967 as a reaction to the trend of the late 1950s and early 1960s to amalgamate everything into large units and in the Midlands to sweep away the area's industrial heritage in the process.

The general aim of the Society is to create interest in the past, present and future of the Black Country, and early on it campaigned for the establishment of an industrial museum. In 1975 the Black Country Museum was started by Dudley Borough Council on 26 acres of totally derelict land adjoining the grounds of Dudley Castle. This has developed into an award-winning museum which attracts over 250,000 visitors annually.

At the Black Country Museum there is a boat dock fully equipped to restore narrow boats of wood and iron and different boats can be seen on the dock throughout the year. From behind the Bottle and Glass Inn visitors can travel on a canal boat into Dudley Canal Tunnel, a memorable journey to see spectacular limestone caverns and the fascinating Castle Mill Basin.

There are over two thousand members of the Black Country Society and all receive the quarterly magazine *The Blackcountryman*, of which over 119 issues have been published since its founding in 1967. In the whole collection there are some 1,700 authoritative articles on all aspects of the Black Country by historians, teachers, researchers, students, subject experts and ordinary folk with an extraordinary story to tell. The whole constitutes a unique resource about the area and is a mine of information for students and researchers who frequently refer to it. Many schools and libraries are subscribers. Three thousand copies of the magazine are printed each quarter. It is non-commercial, and contributors do not receive payment for their articles.

PO Box 71 · Kingswinford · West Midlands DY6 9YN

To order any of these titles please telephone our distributor, Littlehampton Book Services on 01903 72159
For a catalogue of these and our other titles please ring Regina Schinner on 01453 731114